GALE
CENGAGE Learning

Novels for Students, Volume 20

Project Editors: Ira Mark Milne and Timothy Sisler **Editorial**: Anne Marie Hacht, Maikue Vang

Rights Acquisition and Management: Edna Hedblad, Sheila Spencer, Ann Taylor **Manufacturing**: Rhonda Williams

Imaging: Lezlie Light, Mike Logusz, Kelly A. Quin **Product Design**: Pamela A. E. Galbreath

Product Manager: Meggin Condino

For more information, contact
Thomson Gale
27500 Drake Rd.
Farmington Hills, MI 48331-3535
Or you can visit our Internet site at

corrected in future editions.

ISBN 0-7876-6943-1
ISSN 1094-3552

Printed in the United States of America
10 9 8 7 6 5 4 3 2 1

The Wind in the Willows

Kenneth Grahame 1908

Introduction

The Wind in the Willows was published near the turn of the century—1908 in England and 1909 in America. It was based on stories that Kenneth Grahame, the author, told to his son Alastair, starting on Alastair's fourth birthday. The principle characters of these stories are talking animals who live in and around a river, though to the animals, it is "*the* River" (author's emphasis). At the time of the work's publication, Grahame had already published four books of fiction. He was most well known for his collections of stories *The Golden Age* and its sequel *Dream Days*. Though the works were written about children, they were not written for children. *The Wind in the Willows* was not initially well received because it deviated from his previous works; however, it eventually became the work that he is most famous for, enjoyed by children and adults alike.

The principle characters in the novel, though they all have their faults, are idealized in many ways. Several virtues are epitomized in Mole, Rat, Badger, and Toad, so much so that they become themes. There are numerous examples of hospitality, forgiveness, compassion, generosity, and humility. Even the arrogant Toad is able to humble himself and put aside his conceited ways in the end, having matured though a succession of trying circumstances with the guidance and help of loyal friends.

Author Biography

Kenneth Grahame was born in Edinburgh, Scotland, on March 8, 1859, the third of four children to James Cunningham and Bessie Ingles Grahame. When Grahame was just five years old, his mother contracted scarlet fever and died. James Grahame "never recovered from the loss of his wife and did virtually nothing to help his children recover from it," as Kuznets says in *Kenneth Grahame*, and the Grahame children moved with their maternal grandmother, Granny Ingles, to Cookham Dene, a town in Berkshire, along the Thames River.

At age nine, Grahame began school at St. Edward's School in Oxford with his older brother Willie. Here, Grahame excelled at both academics and athletics and still had "time to roam the gardens of Oxford and to continue his loving relationship with the river Thames, which runs through Oxford as it does through Cookham Dene, and indeed through most of Grahame's life," as Kuznets states in her biography. Although Grahame was an accomplished scholar, his family refused to further his education, and at age 16, he ended his schooling and applied for a clerkship at the Bank of England in London.

Banker's hours were short in London, and Grahame participated in the London Scottish Regiment drills, volunteered at Toynbee Hall, served as honorary secretary of the Shakespeare Society, and explored the city and the countryside. Shortly after his father's death in 1887, Grahame began to submit his writing for publication, usually anonymously. His description of the Berkshire Downs, "By a Northern Furrow," was published in December of 1888 and is the first published piece definitively attributed to Grahame. The following decade was a productive one for Grahame's writing. He published *Pagan Papers* (1893), *The Golden Age* (1895), *The Headswoman* (1898), and *Dream Days* (1898), as well as many essays and stories.

On July 22, 1899, the forty-year-old Grahame married Elspeth Thomson, despite the disapproval of their family and friends. Their only child, Alastair, was born on May 12, 1900. In 1906, the Grahames moved back to Cookham Dene, and Grahame commuted to work until he resigned in 1908, citing health problems.

The origin of *The Wind in the Willows* dates back to 1904, when Grahame began telling bedtime stories featuring a mole, a giraffe (later replaced by Toad), and a rat to celebrate Alastair's fourth birthday. After some urging by Constance Smedley of the American magazine *Everybody's,* Grahame collected the stories into a single manuscript. *The Wind in the Willows* was initially rejected by publishers as "it was apparently written for children, not for adults who wanted to reminisce about childhood," as Kuznets says, but was eventually published in 1908. *The Wind in the Willows* became a classic children's book, and A. A. Milne later used the novel as the basis for the play *Toad of Toad Hall*, produced in 1930.

Grahame wrote little after the publication of *The Wind in the Willows*. His next published work after *The Wind in the Willows* was a 1913 essay, "The Fellow That Goes Alone," about the joys of solitude in country life. Grahame enjoyed country living and non-literary pursuits in his later years, but he was troubled by circulatory problems, the strains of his marriage, and the death of their son in 1920. On July 6, 1932, Grahame died in his home in Pangbourne of a cerebral hemorrhage.

Chapter 1: The River Bank

The Wind in the Willows begins with Mole who is spring-cleaning his house when he finds that "something up above was calling him imperiously." Giving in to curiosity, he quickly digs his way to the world above. Everything is new to him. He has not even seen a river before. The first person he makes an acquaintance with is Water Rat, who invites Mole on a boat ride and an impromptu picnic. Rat explains much to Mole about aspects of the world above ground and the River Bank community. After the picnic, they head back upstream towards Rat's hole in the bank of the river. Mole ends up almost tip-ping the boat when he excitedly grabs the sculls (or oars) from Rat, which Rat readily forgives.

Chapter 2: The Open Road

Mole and Rat pay a visit to Mr. Toad. Toad is happy to have the company and pleased to meet Mr. Mole, and he convinces them to join him in a cart and horse trip, which is his latest craze. Their first two days on the road are fairly uneventful. On the third day, they come to their first high road, where they are nearly run down by an automobile moving at high speed. The cart is wrecked from veering off the road. Toad is taken by a new craze—

automobiles—and becomes useless as Mole and Rat deal with the situation. They walk to the nearest town where they catch a train that takes them home.

Chapter 3: The Wild Wood

Mole decides to journey alone to the Wild Wood so he can meet Mr. Badger when he is unable to convince Rat to take him. At first, Mole is not alarmed upon entering the Wild Wood, but he quickly becomes lost and frightened. He ends up hiding in the hollow of a tree. When Rat becomes aware of Mole's absence, he sets out after him. He finds Mole and allows him to rest awhile before heading home. A sudden snowstorm hits in the meantime, making it difficult for them to find their way, and they become lost. Luckily they stumble upon the home of Mr. Badger.

Chapter 4: Mr. Badger

Mr. Badger promptly takes in the lost travelers. He feeds them, gives them dry clothes, and allows them to warm themselves by his fire. Rat fills in Mr. Badger on Toad's automobile craze, and they decide that once the winter has passed, they will "take Toad seriously in hand." Otter also arrives at Mr. Badger's. He explains how the River Bank community has been worried about Rat and Mole being gone. Mole and Badger get more acquainted while they tour the many passages of his home. Badger eventually takes his visitors to the edge of the Wild Wood in one of his extensive passages so that they can get home without further incident.

Media Adaptations

- In 1930, A. A. Milne wrote a successful musical stage version called *Toad of Toad Hall*, which focuses on the adventures of Toad. A. A. Milne is most well-known for his *Winnie-the-Pooh* books.

- Numerous animated film adaptations have been made of *The Wind in the Willows*. One of the earliest and most interesting is the 1949 Disney version entitled *Ichabod and Mr. Toad*, which also included stories from Washington Irving's *Sketch Book of Geoffrey Crayon*. A recent popular version was produced by HBO Studios in 1996.

- Several audio versions of *The Wind in the Willows* have been recorded, including one produced by Naxos on Audio CD in 2002.

Chapter 5: Dulce Domum

Mole has a sudden and almost irresistible urge to see his home again after encountering its smell on a journey. Rat decides that they should go and see it, to Mole's delight. Since he has been away for so long, he doesn't have much for them to eat. A group of field mice stop by to sing carols. Mole is distressed at having nothing to feed them, as he has traditionally done in the past. Rat sends one of the mice off to buy groceries. The mice continue to entertain Mole and Rat until the food arrives, and they have supper. Rat tells Mole that he has a "ripping little house."

Chapter 6: Mr. Toad

Spring arrives, and Rat and Mole are preparing the boat for another season when Badger stops by to tell them that the time has come to intervene with Toad's irresponsible behavior with motorcars. Badger makes an unsuccessful attempt to requite Toad, after which they lock him in his room and guard him "till the poison has worked itself out of his system." Toad manages to escape. He steals a car, smashes it, and ends up in jail.

Chapter 7: The Piper at the Gates of Dawn

Rat, returning from an engagement with the Otters, brings news to Mole of the family's missing child, Portly. They decide to search for the boy by paddling upstream in the boat. Rat starts to hear beautiful music, which Mole is also eventually able to hear. They follow it until they find a mythical creature with horns and hoofed feet, at which lies the lost child, asleep. The creature vanishes, and they take the child to his father. Rat and Mole seem to forget their mythical helper, though they feel a little strange.

Chapter 8: Toad's Adventures

The jailor's daughter takes pity on Toad and devises a plan for his escape that involves disguising him as a washerwoman. Toad is able to attain his freedom but finds that he has rather limited resources since his coat and money, among other things, are still in his jail cell. An engine driver allows Toad aboard his train after being convinced that Toad is "a poor unhappy washerwoman." After riding for several miles, the engine driver realizes that they are being pursued by the police. Toad confesses all to the driver, who still manages to take pity on him. The driver slows down the train at an advantageous point and Toad jumps off. Having evaded his pursuers, he finds himself in an unfamiliar wood.

Chapter 9: Wayfarers All

Rat finds himself restless on a beautiful summer day. He encounters field mice making early preparations for winter as well as swallows who reminisce of their southern winter homes. Rat is thinking about what it would be like to do more traveling when a seafaring rat wanders by. The Sea Rat tells him of his experiences abroad. Upon his departure, the Sea Rat has convinced Rat to come with him. Rat returns home to gather a few things before heading off, but Mole is ultimately able to prevent him from leaving.

Chapter 10: The Further Adventures of Toad

Having spent a night in the unfamiliar wood, Toad is a little cold but happy to be free. He follows a canal and eventually encounters a horse towing a barge with a stout woman aboard. Using his washerwoman outfit to his advantage, he is able to convince the bargewoman to take him aboard. The woman sees through his disguise when Toad is unable to help her with her washing and throws him overboard. Insulted, he steals her horse, which he sells to a gypsy. Still needing a way to get home, he hails a passing motorcar, which turns out to be the car he had stolen earlier. He is not recognized through his disguise. Toad convinces the gentlemen in the car to let him drive for a while. In his excitement at being behind the wheel again, he reveals his identity and ends up smashing the car again. He is once more pursued by the police but escapes when he falls into the swift-moving river and is swept downstream.

Chapter 11: "Like Summer Tempests Came His Tears"

The Water Rat pulls Toad from the water. After telling Rat of his adventures, he gets cleaned up. Rat tells Toad that Toad Hall has been taken over by Stoats and Weasels. Toad, infuriated, attempts to infiltrate his home twice but is repelled by the Stoat guards. Badger arrives at Rat's, having devised a plan that will allow Toad, Rat, Mole, and himself to liberate Toad Hall while the Weasels are enjoying a banquet in celebration of the Chief Weasel's birthday. On the morning they intend to carry out the plan, Mole journeys to Toad Hall alone and, using Toad's washerwomen disguise, beguiles the Stoats into believing that a massive invasion of Badgers, Rats, and Toads would be coming that night.

Chapter 12: The Return of Ulysses

After being outfitted with weapons by Rat, they follow a passage that takes them underneath Toad Hall and into the pantry. The Chief Weasel is in the midst of singing a derisive song about Toad when the four friends spring forth from the pantry, scaring away the Weasels at the banquet and the Stoats outside. The morning after the attack, Badger convinces Toad that he needs to have a banquet to celebrate. Preparations are made and invitations sent out. Shortly before the event, Toad gives a speech and sings a song to an imaginary audience in his room, though he is very humble when the actual guests arrive.

Characters

Badger

Badger, sometimes referred to as Mr. Badger, commands great respect as well as fear among the animals. Rat is the first to mention him: "Dear old Badger! Nobody interferes with *him*. They'd better not." By the end of the novel, he is especially feared by the Weasels, who quiet their infants by telling them that "if they didn't hush them and not fret them, the terrible gray Badger would up and get them." Toad is able to humble himself and apologize for his reckless behavior with automobiles when Badger has him alone in a room. It is only after he is with Rat and Mole again that is able to say "No! … I'm *not* sorry!"

Badger is also considered very wise. He is rarely questioned by Rat and Mole and only occasionally by the arrogant Toad. He is also impartial in his shrewdness. When Toad says "I'll learn 'em to steal my house!" in reference to the Stoats and Weasels, Rat corrects him, replacing "learn" with "teach." However, Badger insists that Toad's manner of speaking is more appropriate. Later, however, when Mole recounts how he visited the Stoat guards in disguise and exaggerated their coming attack, Rat and Toad both reprimand him for giving away the element of surprise while Badger commends him for his cleverness at putting the animals on edge.

Although he is wise, respected, and feared, he is not above being compassionate and forgiving. He is always willing to assist those in need, especially friends. He takes in Mole and Rat without hesitation when they are lost in the Wild Wood. He gives them dry clothes and food and allows them to stay the night. He takes great pains in attempting to get Toad to behave responsibly during his motorcar craze and is still selfless towards him when his efforts do not work. He looks after Toad Hall while Toad is in jail and helps Toad retake his home when it is overrun with Weasels and Stoats.

Bargewoman

Toad meets with the bargewoman shortly after his escape from jail when he is lost in the woods. She is a stout and rather rustic woman. She seems quite willing to assist Toad when she thinks he is a washerwoman that might be able to help her with her laundry, but wastes no time in throwing him overboard when it turns out that he has no skill whatsoever at washing.

Engine Driver

The engine driver seems willing to help anyone in a desperate situation. When Toad is disguised as a washerwoman, he gives Toad a ride on his train because Toad, as the washerwoman, can't get home to see her kids because she has lost her money. When they are later pursued by the police, Toad confesses to his crimes and trickery, but the engine driver is still willing to help him evade his pursuers, saying "… you are evidently in sore trouble and distress, so I will not desert you."

Gentlemen in the Motorcar

The gentlemen with the motorcar mostly serve to move the plot along. The first time they appear in the text, they merely provide Toad with a car to steal. When they appear later on, they pick Toad up on the side of the road and let him try driving their automobile, intrigued by the idea of a washerwoman driving. Toad becomes so elated at being behind the wheel again, after spending so many days in jail, that he gives himself away and also ends up smashing the car. One of the gentlemen, after finding a policeman, pursues Toad across a field until Toad falls into the river, which sweeps him back to the River Bank community.

Gypsy

Toad encounters the gypsy after riding a few miles on the horse he stole from the bargewoman. Finding himself famished, he moves toward a caravan, or covered wagon, beside which are the gypsy and a pot over a fire radiating delicious smells. He goes over to see if he can find a way to get something to eat. The gypsy quickly asks if he can buy Toad's horse. Toad bargains with him and eventually gets six shillings and six pence for it, plus as much of the gypsy's stew as he can eat.

Jailor's Daughter

The jailer, knowing how fond his daughter is of taking care of animals, allows her to take care of Toad upon her request. She brings his meals, which are likely better than what the other inmates get, and she keeps him company. They grow to like each other more and more, so much so that the jailer's daughter can no longer stand seeing Toad locked up. She devises a successful plan for him to escape in which Toad is disguised in the clothes of her aunt, who is the washerwoman for the jail.

Mole

Mole is arguably the most passionate of all of *The Wind in the Willows* characters. He is always willing to help another animal in need. Even when Rat, a rather compassionate character himself, is not able to muster the initiative to go looking for the Otter family's lost child, Portly, Mole insists they do something, saying "I simply can't go and turn in, and go to sleep, and *do* nothing, even though there doesn't seem to be anything to be done." Mole is generally very excited about people, whether meeting them for the first time, or seeing them after a long absence. When Toad returns home from his "adventures," Badger is somewhat sympathetic in his greeting, but a little too reserved for Toad's liking, while Mole is ecstatic at seeing him and gives Toad exactly the type of greeting he wants, telling him that he is a "clever, ingenious, intelligent Toad!" Mole's emotions are stirred by more than just people. When seeing Rat's boat for the first time, his "whole heart went out to it at once...."

Mole is new to the River Bank community and to the entire world above ground. In the beginning of the novel, he is much like a child, seeing everything for the first time, as demonstrated when he says to Rat, "all this is so new to me. So—this—is—a—River!" He is very eager to do and experience new things, as when he grabs the oars from Rat in order to try rowing. He is quite astute, quickly picking up skills and subtle intuitions, as demonstrated in the following lines:

He learnt to swim and to row, and entered into the joy of running water; and with his ear to the reed stems he caught, at intervals, something of what the wind went whispering so constantly among them.

Mole is also rather independent for someone so new to the area, which gets him into trouble at the beginning of the novel. In his usual manner, he is very anxious to meet Mr. Badger, whom he's heard much about from Rat. Rat, who is content to wait for Badger to call on them, is too passive for him. Mole decides he will venture into the Wild Wood alone in order to meet Badger, which leads to him getting lost and stuck in a snowstorm. But he does get to meet Badger before his journey is over. Toward the end of the novel, Mole again ventures out alone in disguise and convinces the Stoats that a massive attack is coming to Toad Hall. This makes their small ambush more effective and also shows how much wiser he has become in the ways of the above ground world.

Otter

Otter is a good friend of the novel's four main characters, Rat, Mole, Badger, and Toad, and comes into the story several times in person and by name. He often serves as a link to the River Bank community at large. Upon his first appearance in the text, he says, "All the world seems out on the river today. I came up this backwater to try to get a moment's peace, and then stumble upon you fellows!" There are several more occurrences of Otter bringing information from the larger community into the reader's scope, another important one being when he arrives at Badger's house and describes how the community was alarmed that Rat and Mole were missing.

Otter is also distinct in that he has the closest thing to a representation of a family in the book. The four main characters are all bachelors. Otter not only has a son, Portly, but seems to have a family, which is referred to as "the Otters." The Otters are never specifically called a family, but it is clearly implied by the fact that they entertain Rat at their house as a unit and inquire about Portly as a unit.

Portly

While Portly does not affect the overall events in *The Wind in the Willows*, he is central to chapter

7, "The Piper at the Gates of Dawn." Portly is Otter's son and is so young that he is referred to as a baby at one point. Portly has a tendency to wonder off alone, which is usually not a worrisome event since everyone in the River Bank knows and looks after him. In this chapter, however, he is gone for multiple days, which causes the Otters a certain amount of anxiety. Rat and Mole find him at the feet of a mythological creature, presumably the "piper" mentioned in the chapter title, by following his music. Portly is not mentioned elsewhere in the book, which is in keeping with this anomalous chapter that also presents the one-time development of magic as well as the strongest development of a character's family, i.e., the Otters.

Rat

Rat, also known as River Rat, is one of the four central figures in the novel. One of the first noticeable characteristics about Rat is his generosity. He is the first person that Mole meets above ground, and Rat welcomes him to the River Bank by taking him on a boat ride and bringing along a picnic for them to share, which includes "coldtonguecoldhamcoldbeefpickledgherkinssal adfrenchrollscresssandwichespottedmeatginger beerlemonadesodawater —." Coming home after the picnic, Rat invites Mole to stay at his house for the night. The novel spans roughly a year, and Mole lives in Rat's house for almost that entire time. One of the few exceptions is when they stay at Mole's house for a night, and even then, Rat demonstrates his generosity by giving one of the field mice money to buy groceries for a nice supper, allowing Mole to be a good host to his visitors.

Rat is also a compassionate character, though he seems to be more inclined to help others when it is a matter of proper appearance or behavior. When he finds Mole after he wandered off alone in the Wild Wood, the first thing Rat says to him is, "You shouldn't really have gone and done it.... We riverbankers, we hardly ever come here by ourselves." When he pulls Toad from the river after he has escaped the police, he immediately tells him to "go off upstairs at once … and put on some of my clothes and try and come down looking like a gentleman." This may explain why he is at first inclined to do nothing when young Portly goes missing. He may feel helpless since solving the problem has nothing to do with instilling proper animal behavior.

Sea Rat

The Sea Rat is another character that is central to one chapter, "Wayfarers All," but appears no where else in the text. Rat encounters the Sea Rat one day when he is feeling restless, and he doesn't know why. The Sea Rat tells Rat of his adventures abroad. Rat is swept away in his stories and intends to go with the Sea Rat to his next destination, but he is stopped by Mole. The encounter with the Sea Rat enhances one of themes of the novel—the struggle between a desire to indulge in the familiarity of home and the desire to experience new things away from home.

Stoats and Weasels

The Stoats and Weasels take over Toad Hall while Toad is in jail, to the surprise of Badger and Mole who are looking after it. Rat tells Toad how "they took and beat them severely with sticks … and turned them out into the cold…." They are theantagonists for the last two chapters of *The Wind in the Willows*, "'Like Summer Tempests Came His Tears,'" and "The Return of Ulysses." However, they are more complex than that, as Rat explains: "They're all right in a way—I'm very good friends with them … but they break out sometimes … and then—well, you can't really trust them…." In keeping with Rat's description, one of the Weasels, shortly after being expelled, comes back to Toad Hall to see if he can be of service in any way.

Toad

Toad is the driving force for the plot twists of a large portion of the book. His automobile craze leads to him stealing a car and getting sentenced to twenty years in prison. He escapes from prison and returns home, being periodically pursued by the police on the way. As he journeys home, he meets several interesting people, including the engine driver, the bargewoman, and the gypsy. He eventually finds himself at Rat's house, who tells him that the Stoats and Weasels have taken over his house. Thus the four principle characters must join together to recapture Toad Hall.

Rat gives a fairly accurate description of Toad's personality, though he is probably being a little too kind:

So simple, so good-natured, and so affectionate. Perhaps he's not very clever—we can't all be geniuses; and it may be that he is both boastful and conceited. But he has got some great qualities, has Toady.

Toad does enjoy a simple life. Having inherited a great amount of wealth, he does not have to work to provide for himself. Instead he is constantly looking to fill his life with whatever hobby most captures his attention at the time. He also enjoys entertaining and will often try to combine entertaining his friends with his hobbies, which leads to the cart trip with Mole and Rat. Toad is also indeed arrogant and enjoys being the center of attention. He often dreams of delivering speeches and singing songs describing his exploits to a captivated audience, as he pretends to do just before the party celebrating the recapture of Toad Hall. In the very end, Toad seems to have mended his ways, no longer acting so arrogant and self-centered. As the text indicates, "He was indeed an altered Toad!"

Hospitality

Hospitality comes naturally to many of the characters in *The Wind in the Willows*. The text is filled with occurrences of one animal offering food and/or shelter to another. At times it is merely a casual exchange among friends, like Rat's long standing engagement of going to the Otters' for dinner, or Rat paying a call on Toad and introducing his friend Mole. At other times, there is a specific need, as when Badger brings Rat and Mole out of the cold of a snowstorm, followed by a pair of lost hedgehogs the next morning. The novel's most impressive example of hospitality is that of Rat taking Mole into his home, which ends up lasting at least a year, having only met Mole that day. There is neither discussion of payment nor any sort of anticipation that Mole will return the favor. It is simply accepted. Shortly after Mole is invited to stay at Rat's, the text reads, "When they got home, the Rat made a bright fire in the parlor...." It does not say "when they got to Rat's home" because it is now home to them both.

Forgiveness

Forgiveness comes quickly and easily in *The Wind in the Willows*, regardless of the size the offense. When Mole apologizes to Rat for taking the sculls away from him in the boat, which leads to Mole and the luncheon basket going overboard, Rat immediately responds with "That's all right, bless you!" He then goes on to invite Mole to stay with him awhile so that he can learn to row and swim.

Toad is forgiven several times throughout the book for much more serious misconduct. Even four Weasels, taken prisoner during the recapture of Toad Hall, are treated kindly when they demonstrate contrition: "They were very penitent, and said they were extremely sorry…. So I [Mole] gavethem a roll apiece, and let them out at the back, and off they ran." Toad is also able to let bygones be bygones when one of the Weasels returns to Toad Hall looking to be of service. It is only with the slightest condescension that he pats the Weasel on the head and gives him an errand to run.

Humility

While there are not obvious examples of humility throughout the text, it is a major theme because it is a virtue that one of the principle characters, Toad, clearly does not possess but clearly needs to learn. His friends are very patient with him as he, time and time again, embarrasses them by making a fool of himself. As Rat says, "Do you suppose it is any pleasure for me … to hear animals saying … that I'm the chap that keeps company with jailbirds?"

In the end, after a series of trying circumstances that Toad manages to fare only through the kindness of strangers and the loyalty of his friends, he is finally able to humble himself. Even when Otter encourages him during the celebration of the recapture of Toad Hall, Toad responds with "I merely served in the ranks and did little or nothing."

Topics for Further Study

- Grahame focuses on the mammals, and one amphibian, that live in and around a river. What else can be found in a riverbank ecosystem? Write a 500-word essay considering Grahame's depiction of a riverbank as it compares with actual river ecology.

- Read *Animal Farm*, by George Orwell. How does his use of anthropomorphized animals differ from that of Grahame's? How are they similar? What sort of literary devices does each take advantage of through the use of animals?

- Read or attend a performance of A. A. Milne's *Toad of Toad Hall*. Milne did not cover the events of all the chapters in *The Wind in the Willows*. Identify a chapter that was omitted by Milne. Write a stage version of that chapter and direct a performance of it.

- What literary work is Grahame referring to when he titles the final chapter of *The Wind in the Willows* The Return of Ulysses? What parallels can be made between Toad and the protagonist of this literary work?

Compassion

The events of *The Wind in the Willows* are often shaped by characters helping other characters. Toad is most frequently the person in need of assistance. His friends Badger, Mole, and Rat are always there for him, whether they are locking him in a room in order to cure him of his automobile craze or putting together a plan to drive the Stoats and Weasels out of Toad Hall. Toad's escape from prison would have been impossible if it wasn't for the kindness of complete strangers. The jailor's daughter takes pity on Toad merely because she hates to see animals suffer. The engine driver helps Toad upon their first meeting, both when he thinks Toad is a washerwoman and when he is aware that he is a Toad on the run from the law. The gentlemen that Toad steals the car from are a little too angry to help Toad as Toad, but they do not hesitate to help him when he is disguised as the washerwoman.

Toad is not the only one who gets himself into trouble. As soon as Rat realizes that Mole has gotten himself lost in the Wild Wood, he starts out after him. When Rat and Mole both end up lost in the snowstorm, Badger keeps them from freezing by taking them into his home. Otter, also worried about Rat and Mole, comes to find them at Badger's and offers to guide them home. Rat and Mole are able to return the favor when they find Otter's son Portly when he goes missing.

Home

A tension exists in *The Wind in the Willows* between the desire to stay near the comforts of home and the urge to see and explore new places. In the very beginning, Mole, tired of spring-cleaning, decides to leave his home. "Something up above was calling him imperiously." For nearly all of the rest of the novel, Mole lives away from his underground dwelling, returning only once, again, at the beckon of an overwhelming urge: "the wafts from his old home pleaded, whispered, conjured, and finally claimed him imperiously." The same word is used to describe both urges —"imperiously"—possibly to indicate the parallel strength of their call.

Rat also struggles within this dichotomy. He is generally a person that enjoys being home; both on the cart trip with Toad and when visiting Badger's house, his desire to return to his hole in the riverbank is explicitly indicated. Nonetheless, in the chapter entitled "Wayfarers All," he is determined to partake of the adventures described by the Sea Rat. It is only by force that he is he prevented from leaving.

As demonstrated by the recapture of Toad Hall, home is something worth fighting for. Yet Toad, probably more than any of the principle characters, is afflicted by a powerful wanderlust, which is apparent when he coaxes Rat before the cart trip:

You surely don't mean to stick to your dull fusty old river all your life, and just live in a hole in a bank, and *boat*? I want to show you the world! I'm going to make an *animal* of you, my boy!

By the end of the book, there is no reason to believe that Rat, Toad, and Badger have not returned to their homes. As for Mole, it is not specified whether he continues to live with Rat or goes back to his own quaint lodgings. The "joy and contentment" they all find is not contingent on whether they live near or far away from their home. *The Wind in the Willows* shows the appeal of either possibility but not which one to choose.

Style

Golden Age of Children's Literature

The Golden Age of children's literature has been defined as lasting from the publication of Lewis Carroll's *Alice's Adventures in Wonderland* in 1865 until World War I. Before that time, literature written for children was primarily considered a didactic tool, leaving little room for the imagination. During the Golden Age, the imaginative aspect of children's literature blossomed. The works within the genre were more readily enjoyed by children.

Scholars consider *The Wind in the Willows* to be a contributor to the Golden Age, published near the period's end. Though it may be valued for the examples the animals provide to children with their loyal friendships and displays of hospitality and compassion, its primary purpose is to entertain, in true Golden Age form.

Animal Novel

The tradition of using anthropomorphized animals in both oral and written storytelling is quite old and worldwide spread. Up until the Golden Age, its usual form was the animal fable: short tales in which anthropomorphized animals are used to parody or otherwise criticize human failings. These were often archetypal characters with one or two dominant attributes. One of the most common archetypes is the trickster, an example of which is the Big Bad Wolf from the story of Little Red Riding Hood. The characters in *The Wind in the Willows* are not archetypes, nor is the novel allegorical like fables. As Kuznets points out in her biography of Grahame:

The Wind in the Willows is a book of fair length, with well-developed animal protagonists, who participate in a similarly well-developed plot, built on conflict, both internal and external, to some resolution of those conflicts.

This defies the form of the fable, and, in fact, shares more characteristics with the novel, which is intended for entertainment rather than moral instruction. It was in fact, one of the first animal novels, which paved the way for others to come, such as *Charlotte's Web*, published in 1952, or more recently, *Redwall*, published in 1986.

Historical Context

Grahame was born during the Victorian Era, when the British Empire was at its peak. Its financial institutions were strong and stable. Their manufacturing industries were ever-growing. However, right about the time the first major tragedies were occurring in Grahame's life—the death of his mother at age five and his father's desertion of his family when Grahame was eight—Britain found that its stable roots were being shaken. The Crimean war with Russia from 1854 to 1856 had already cast doubt on England's military strength. Threats of war with Germany, France, Russia, and even the United States compromised overall confidence in the Empire.

British society was also stressed by unrest and fluctuation. In 1870, educational reform brought literacy to the working classes, allowing them to expand their awareness within the political, intellectual, and literary arenas, shifting focus and power away from the old land-owning families. The Trade Union Amendment Act of 1876 gave legal sanction to trade unions, leading to dissatisfaction among industries and major strikes in the 1880s and 1890s. In the beginning of the twentieth century, laborers found a major political voice with the formation of the Labour Party, which is still one of the two main political parties in England to this day. Education reform continued with the founding of the Worker's Education Association in 1903. The roots of the Irish independence movement were also established around this time.

The women's movement contributed to this period of social upheaval. Britain's male-dominated society, though oppressive to half of the population, had maintained a certain amount of stability in the early part of the Victorian age. When liberation organizations established themselves, like the National Union of Women's Suffrage Societies in 1897, the Woman's Social and Political Union in 1903, and the Women's Freedom League in 1908, the male-dominated status quo began to break down.

Compare & Contrast

- **1908:** The speed limit for automobiles is 20 miles per hour (mph) in England. Automobiles are found mostly in Western Europe and North America.
  Today: The speed limit for automobiles in England is as high 70 mph, though it is not uncommon for the flow of traffic to move at 80 mph. Automobiles are found in virtually every country in the world.

- **1908:** The population of the Great Britain is approximately 40,000,000.
  Today: The population of Great Britain is approximately 60,000,000. While this is a 50 percent growth,

roads and urban development have increased at a drastically higher rate, countered by a sharp decrease in cultivated and undeveloped land.

- **1908:** Women in Great Britain do not have the right to vote and have little political power in general, especially with the death of Queen Victoria in 1901 and the ascension of King Edward VII to the throne.

  Today: Women over the age of thirty have had the right to vote since 1918, with women over the age of twenty-one gaining the right in 1928. Women occupy many high level political positions, including seats in the parliament. Margaret Thatcher was elected prime minister in 1979. The monarchy is again occupied by a woman, Queen Elizabeth II.

Changes were occurring throughout England, not just in the cities and industrial areas, but also in the countryside. The rural life was diminishing as urbanization spread. According to Peter Hunt in *The Wind in the Willows: A Fragmented Arcadia*, the last three decades of the nineteenth century saw Britain's cultivated land reduce by half. Railroad lines crisscrossed England as well as roadways, with the automobile becoming more and more popular. Not only was the countryside disappearing, but it was becoming less pristine and much more easily accessible.

Hunt suggests that all these changes gave rise to a nostalgic attitude toward the Victorian life-style that was reflected in some of the literature of the times: "the post-Romantic fashions of the Victorian age became more and more 'precious' and, by Victorian standards, corrupt." He goes on to explain that these writers "would look 'inward' but they also looked out to the countryside, to an arcadian past...."

Grahame was among these writers. As Kuznets quotes in her article "Kenneth Grahame and Father Nature, or Whither Blows *The Wind in the Willows*?" Grahame once said to his Scribner's editor that he wanted to write a book that was "free of problems, clear of the clash of sex." Grahame certainly had his share of problems in his lifetime, not only during his childhood, but also later with an unhappy marriage, and a nearly blind son. *The Wind in the Willows* was a window to a simpler place and a simpler life: a life "clear of the clash of sex," and thus no unhappy marriages and no women's movements disrupting a male-dominated society: a life "free of problems," where children don't have disabilities, and where a child may sometimes get lost but is found again through the help of a magical piper: a place where there are no wars, but only the occasional skirmishes with Stoats and Weasels, who are repentant enough the next morning to get pats on the head: most importantly, a place where a small riverbank community is still intact, pristine, and buffered from the world at large by an untamed wood.

Critical Overview

Grahame at first had trouble placing *The Wind in the Willows* with a publisher. His English editor, John Lane, rejected the manuscript, as did *Everybody's*, the American periodical that initially solicited it. It was finally picked up in 1908 by Methuen in England. Methuen was still skeptical; so much so that he would not pay an advance on it, though Curtis Brow, Grahame's literary agent, was able to get him to agree to rising royalties. In 1909, Scribner published the book in America, but only after receiving a letter from President Theodore Roosevelt in its praise.

Critics did not receive Grahame's new work favorably. After publishing *The Golden Age* in 1895 and its sequel, *Dream Days*, in 1898, both to wide acclaim, his readers were in anticipation of another book involving the Gold Age children. As Peter Hunt puts it in *The Wind in the Willows: A Fragmented Arcadia*: "Kenneth Grahame had been a famous and much-admired writer *about* children, and here, it seemed, was a book *for* children...." It was flouted as an "animal fable," as Lois Kuznets points out in *Kenneth Grahame*. As Grahame's audience adapted and began to appreciate the novel for what it was, its success slowly came to fruition. By 1959, Peter Green reports, in his well-known biography of Grahame, that "*The Wind in the Willows* has achieved over a hundred editions, and an average sale of about 80,000 copies." Its success has continued to grow since. It is now, without a doubt, considered a classic of children's literature.

What Do I Read Next?

- Grahame's *The Golden Age* (1895) is a collection of stories about five imaginative children retreating from their repressive families and into their own fantasies. This work made Grahame famous.

- *Dream Days* (1898) is another collection of stories by Grahame. It is the sequel to *The Golden Age*, involving the same five children. It furthered Grahame's success as a writer.

- *Charlotte's Web* (1952) by E. B. White, like *The Wind in the Willows*, is a novel featuring animal protagonists. In it a pig is saved from being slaughtered through the efforts of a spider who writes words in her web.

- *Redwall* (1986) by Brian Jacques is an animal novel that tells a magical and adventuresome story in which a civilization of rats plays out the age-old conflict of good versus evil. This is the beginning of an entire series of books.

- Several abridged versions of *The Wind in the Willows* have appeared over the years. Joan Collins adapted it into a fifty-two-page "retold for easy reading" version, which was published in Britain in 1983 by Ladybird Books. Bob Blaisdell adapted it into a slightly longer version, which was published in 1995 by Dover publications.

- Several sequels were written by William Horwood, which are entitled *The Willows in the Winter* (1993), *Toad Triumphant* (1995), and *The Willows and Beyond* (1996).

Sources

Gaarden, Bonnie, "The Inner Family of *The Wind in the Willows*," in *Children's Literature: Annual of The Modern Division of Children's Literature and The Children's Literature Association*, Vol. 22, 1994, pp. 43–44, 46.

Grahame, Kenneth, *The Wind in the Willows*, Grosset & Dunlap, 1966, p. 11-221.

Green, Peter, *Kenneth Grahame: A Biography*, World Publishing, 1959, p. 1.

Hunt, Peter, *"The Wind in the Willows": A Fragmented Arcadia*, Twayne Publishers, 1994, pp. 5, 6, 13.

Kuznets, Lois R., *Kenneth Grahame*, Twayne Publishers, 1987, pp. 2, 4, 15, 97, 124, 126.

——, "Kenneth Grahame and Father Nature, or Whither Blows *The Wind in the Willows*?" in *Children's Literature: Annual of The Modern Division of Children's Literature and The Children's Literature Association*, Vol. 16, 1988, p. 175.

Marshall, Cynthia, "Bodies and Pleasures in *The Wind in the Willows*," in *Children's Literature: Annual of The Modern Division of Children's Literature and The Children's Literature Association*, Vol. 22, 1994, p. 60.

Further Reading

Bate, Roger, and Keith Hartley, *Saving Our Streams: The Role of the Anglers' Conservation Association in Protecting English & Welsh Rivers*, Institute of Economic Affairs, 2001.

> Bate and Hartley consider the Anglers' Conservation Association's fight to clean up and preserve English and Welsh rivers that have been damaged through urban development and pollution. The legislation affecting the conservation of river-based ecosystems, also know as riparian systems, is also examined.

Carpenter, Humphrey, *Secret Gardens: A Study of the Golden Age of Children's Literature*, Pubs Overstock, 1991.

> The book examines works from the golden age of children's literature and their authors, including the sources of their inspiration and the cultural circumstances that led these authors to direct their writing towards children.

Eckermann, Erik, and Peter L. Albrecht, *World History of Automobiles*, Society of Automotive Engineers, 2001.

> Eckermann and Albrecht describe

the development of the automobile, from what lead to its invention to the most recent technological advances. Photographs and diagrams complement the text.

Green, Peter, *Kenneth Grahame: A Biography*, World Publishing, 1959.

The earliest comprehensive biography of Grahame, Green's biography is the one most commonly referenced by literary scholars. The book is accompanied by twenty-two pictures and illustrations.

www.ingramcontent.com/pod-product-compliance
Ingram Content Group UK Ltd.
Pitfield, Milton Keynes, MK11 3LW, UK
UKHW020635160925
7919UKWH00040B/702